Fun Ways to Learn the Whole Story of Jesus and His Love

The Names of Jesus

Life and Lessons of Jesus Series

Creative Bible-Learning
Activities for Children
Ages 6-12

The buyer of this book may reproduce pages for classroom or home use.
Duplication for any other use is prohibited without written permission from David C. Cook Publishing Co.

Copyright © 1991 by Tracy Leffingwell Harrast. Published by David C. Cook Publishing Co.
Printed in the United States of America.

Scripture taken from the Holy Bible, New International Version, Copyright © 1973,
1978, 1984 International Bible Society.
Used by permission of Zondervan Bible Publishers.

Book Design by Tabb Associates
Cover Illustration by Gary Locke
Interior Illustrations by Anne Kennedy

THIS BOOK BELONGS TO:

_____

To My Children and Others Who Read This Book

"Who do you say I am?" That's an important question Jesus asked Peter (Matthew 16:15; Luke 9:20). Who do you say Jesus is? He wants to be your Savior, your Lord, and more.

Jesus said, "Learn from me" (Matthew 11:29). As you learn about Him, pray from your heart and listen carefully during your prayers every day. You'll come to know His voice (John 10:4) and you'll find Him to be everything the Bible says He is. Instead of just knowing *about* Him, you will really *know* Him.

—Tracy L. Harrast

The Names of Jesus
CONTENTS

Seek and You Will Find 5

Add a Line 6

Alpha and Omega (John 1:1-3; Revelation 11:6, 15; 22:13) 7

The Bread of Life (John 6:31-58) 8-9

The Bridegroom (Matthew 9:15; 22:1-10; 25:1-13; Mark 2:19, 20; Luke 12:35-38) 10-12

The Christ (Acts 4:27; 10:38; Hebrews 1:9) 13

Commander (Joshua 5:13-15, Isaiah 55:4; Romans 11:26; Ephesians 6:10-12) 14

The Chief Cornerstone (Matthew 21:42; Mark 12:10; Luke 20:17; Acts 4:11;
    I Corinthians 3:11; Ephesians 2:19-22; I Peter 2:6) 15

Friend (Matthew 28:20; Luke 15:1, 2; John 15:13, 15) 16

The Gate (John 10:1, 9; 14:6) 17-18

Gift of God (John 3:16; 4:10; Romans 6:23; II Corinthians 9:15) 19

God (Exodus 3:13, 14; John 5:18; 8:58, 59; 10:30) 20

Immanuel (Matthew 1:23) 21

Jesus (Matthew 1:20, 21; Luke 2:30; Acts 4:12; Philippians 2:9) 22-23

The King of Kings (Matthew 28:18; John 3:3-5; Kingdom Parables) 24-25

The Lamb of God (John 1:29; Hebrews 9:7, 11-14) 26

The Light (John 1:4, 5, 9; 3:19-21; 8:12; 12:35, 36, 46) 27

The Lord (Matthew 10:39; Mark 8:34-37; Luke 6:46-49; 9:23, 24) 28-29

The Mediator (Romans 5:11, 18; I Timothy 2:5) 30

The Messiah (Old Testament Prophecies & New Testament Fulfillments) 31

The Great Physician (Matthew 8:14, 15; 9:1-8; Mark 5:21-24, 35-43;
    10:46-52; Luke 5:17-25; 7:11-15; 17:11-19; John 11:1-53) 32

The Redeemer (Matthew 20:28; Mark 10:45; John 8:31, 32, 34, 36; I Timothy 2:6) 33

The Resurrection and the Life (John 11:25, 26) 34

The Rock (John 4:13, 14; 7:37-39; I Corinthians 10:4) 35

The Savior (Matthew 10:22; 24:13; 4:12; Romans 10:9, 10, 13; Ephesians 2:8) 36

Servant (Luke 22:26, 27; John 13:4-15) 37

The Good Shepherd (John 10:14-16, 27-30) 38

The Son of God (Matthew 3:17; 17:1-8; Mark 1:11; 9:2-8; Luke 9:28-36) 39

The True Vine (John 15:5, 8) 40

The Way (John 14:6; Ephesians 2:8, 9) 41

The Word (John 1:1-3) 42

Answers 43-44

I DID IT! 45

Index of Life and Lessons of Jesus Series 46-47

Write the Author 48

Seek and You Will Find

Find these names of Jesus in the puzzle and circle them.

ALPHA AND OMEGA	GATE	PASSOVER LAMB
BREAD OF LIFE	I AM	REDEEMER
CHRIST	JESUS	SAVIOR
DELIVERER	KING OF KINGS	TEACHER
IMMANUEL	LIGHT	VINE
FRIEND	MESSIAH	WORD

```
L I G H T R G I A M S U S E J
C B W O R D V I N E R O I V A
R O I V A S N E C S V K L T R
P F E S N R B A H S A F L D C
A L Y A R E J K R I M R A E H
S D Y L N O L I I A Y I U L E
S R E H T A E H S H J E R I R
O N L Y B E G O T T E N E V Y
V I M M A N U E L H H D N E L
E M Y C N A N L K S D A B R M
R E D E E M E R G I O I T E I
L L E R R E T K R A M W E R J
A L P H A A N D O M E G A T E
M Y C N A N R O B I N M C L H
B R E A D O F L I F E S H G S
Y B U R D L G C N O V D E T O
S S G N I K F O G N I K R F J
```

Add a Line

Here's your big chance to be a detective! See if you can figure out what the shapes below say. *Add one line to each of the shapes to form a letter. The letters make names of Jesus. If you need help, look at the contents on pages 3-4 to see some of Jesus' names. Have fun!*

1. SAVIOR
2. MESSIAH
3. BREAD OF LIFE
4. FRIEND
5. GOD
6. LORD
7. SON OF GOD
8. KING OF KINGS
9. LORD
10. REDEEMER

Alpha and Omega

Jesus said, "I am the Alpha and the Omega, the First and the Last, the Beginning and the End." Alpha and omega are the first and last letters of the Greek alphabet. In English, Jesus would be saying He is the A and the Z.

Jesus' life didn't begin when He was born in Bethlehem, and it didn't end when He was crucified. Jesus was with the Father when time began, and He will be with the Father when time ends.

Alpha and Omega Book Rack

Jesus knows what's in every book that was ever written. He has seen everything that has happened in the past, and He can see everything that will happen in the future. Make this book rack to remind you of all that Jesus knows.

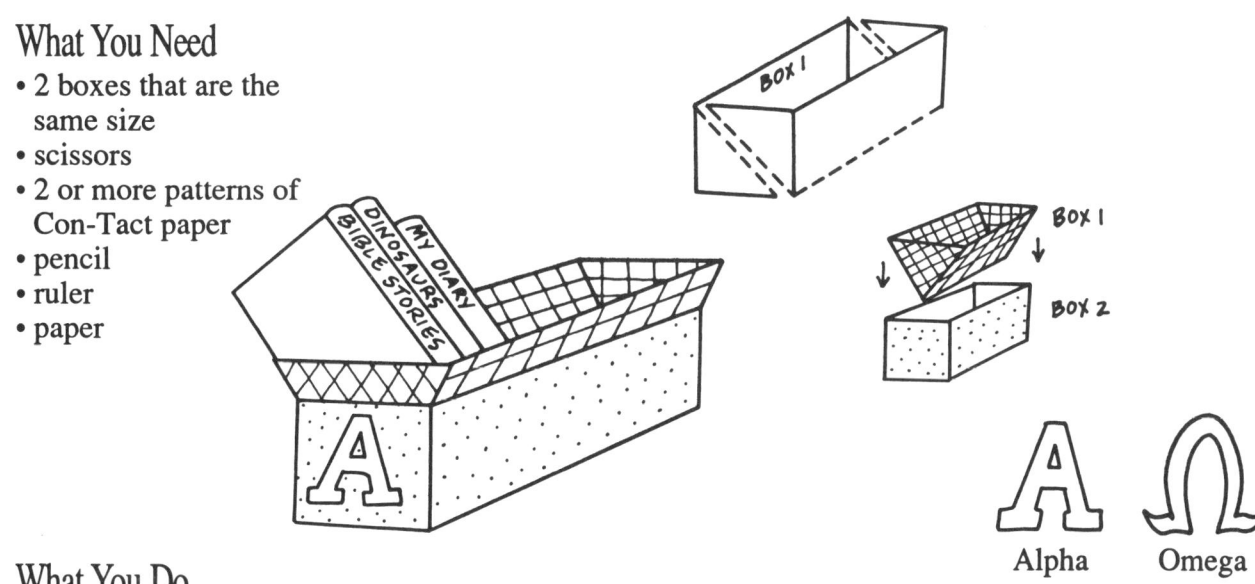

What You Need
- 2 boxes that are the same size
- scissors
- 2 or more patterns of Con-Tact paper
- pencil
- ruler
- paper

Alpha   Omega

What You Do
1. On one narrow end of box 1, draw a line from the top left corner to the bottom right corner. On the other narrow end of the box, draw a line from the top right corner to the bottom left corner.
2. Cut along the lines and along the crease as shown so that you have a triangle-shaped box.
3. Cover both boxes with patterned Con-Tact paper, using a different pattern for each box. Put box 1 inside box 2 as shown.
4. Draw an alpha and an omega on Con-Tact paper different from box 2, and cut them out.
5. Remove the backing from the alpha and attach it to one end of box 2. Remove the backing from the omega and attach it to the other end of box 2. Now you can fill your rack with books!

Draw a star in this box when you've read John 1:1-3; and Revelation 11:6, 15; 22:13.

The Bread of Life

After Moses and the Israelites left Egypt, they wandered around in the wilderness for forty years. During that time, God sent a breadlike food called manna from heaven each day to keep them alive. Jesus said that He is the living bread that came down from heaven that will keep us alive for eternity!

Decode three ways that Jesus is like manna.

1. Fill in the missing vowels. The vowels are A, E, I, O, and U.
P_ _pl_ w_nt t_ kn_w G_d _nd b_ sur_
th_y w_ll g_t t_ l_v_ w_th H_m f_r_v_r.
Wh_n th_y p_t th_ _r tr_st _n J_s_s, H_ s_t_sf_ _s
th_t h_ng_r l_k_ th_ m_nn_ s_t_sf_ _d th_ h_ng_r _f
th_ _sr_ _l_t_s.

2. It's as easy to read as 1, 2, 3! To find out what these numbers are trying to say, replace each number with the letter that holds its place in the alphabet.
1=A, 2=B, 3=C, 4=D, 5=E, 6=F, 7=G, 8=H, 9=I, 10=J, 11=K, 12=L, 13=M, 14=N, 15=O, 16=P, 17=Q, 18=R, 19=S, 20=T, 21=U, 22=V, 23=W, 24=X, 25=Y, 26=Z

20/8/5   9/19/18/1/5/12/9/20/5/19   23/15/21/12/4   8/1/22/5   4/9/5/4   9/6

7/15/4   8/1/4   14/15/20   19/5/14/20   13/1/14/14/1.   23/5   23/15/21/12/4

1/12/12   4/9/5   6/15/18   5/20/5/18/14/9/20/25   9/6   7/15/4   8/1/4   14/15/20

19/5/14/20   10/5/19/21/19.

3. Looks like someone's typewriter had the hiccups! To decode this message, correct the spacing between the words.

TheIsr aeli teshad toco llect the irma nna ev eryd ay.Wen eedto prayev eryd ayandke ep tr usti nginJe sus.

Draw a star in this box when you've read John 6:31-58.

8

Make Bread Words

Jesus said, "I am the bread of life." You can write about the Bread of Life by following this recipe!

What You Need
- grown-up help
- frozen bread dough
- shortening
- egg white
- 1 teaspoon water
- coarse kosher salt

Jesus is the Bread of Life

What You Do
1. Thaw the dough.
2. Have a grown-up preheat the oven to the temperature recommended on the bread dough package.
3. Shape the dough into letters and put them on a greased cookie sheet.
4. Mix the egg white with water and brush onto the letters.
5. Sprinkle with coarse kosher salt.
6. Bake until golden brown. Watch carefully, because this will bake much faster than the package says it would take for a loaf to bake. (Be sure to have a grown-up help you put your bread into the oven and take it out.)

☐ *Draw a star in this box when you've read John 6:48.*

The Bridegroom

Jesus called Himself the Bridegroom. A bridegroom is a man who is getting married. In Bible times, people became betrothed before they got married. When they got betrothed, they would make marriage promises and then later they would hold a wedding dinner and celebration.

Jesus is a Bridegroom to everyone who believes in Him. He has promised to come back and take His believers to their new home in heaven, just as a bridegroom takes his bride to live with him. For those who love Jesus, it will be a time of great celebration.

One day Jesus told this story about a wedding feast to show how God calls people to be in His kingdom.

Be Ready for the Bridegroom

Fill in each blank with the correct word from the following list. You can check your answers in Luke 12:35-38.

door
wedding
table
master
lamps
servants
service
knocks
watching
good

Be dressed ready for 1._____ and keep your 2._____ burning, like men waiting for their master to return from a 3._____ banquet, so that when he comes and 4._____ they can immediately open the 5._____ for him. It will be good for those 6._____ whose master finds them 7._____ when he comes. I tell you the truth, he will dress himself to serve, will have them recline at the 8._____ and will come and wait on them. It will be 9._____ for those servants whose 10._____ finds them ready, even if he comes [very late at night].

Draw a star in this box when you've read Luke 12:35-38.

The Wedding Feast

A 👑 thr + 👞-sh A wedding 🍽 4 his 🌞. The 👥 🦉 were invited would 🐛 come when the 👑's helpers went to c+ 🏐 -B them. They 😂 +ed 🦇 -B the helpers & even killed them! The 👑 S + ⛺ -T his 👊 +Y 2 🔥 th+ 🐻 -B city. Then the 👑 S+ ⛺ -T his helpers 2 ask every 1 else 2 the wedding.

---

1. Which picture in the story was God? Draw it here.

2. Which picture in the story was Jesus? Draw it here.

☐ *Draw a star in this box when you've read Matthew 9:15; 22:1-10; Mark 2:19, 20; Luke 5:34, 35.*

Ten Young Women with Lamps

In Bible times, people didn't have electric lights like we have today. They filled a lamp with oil and put a wick in it. If there was no oil, the lamp wouldn't burn.

Jesus liked to teach people things by telling them a story. Here is a story He told that has a word missing from each line. To complete the story, put a ∧ mark on each line to show where the word at the beginning of the line belongs. (In line one, the word *ten* belongs before *young*.)

ten	The kingdom of heaven is like ∧ young women who took their lamps
wise	and went to meet the bridegroom. Five of them were and five were
oil	foolish. The foolish ones brought lamps without extra, but the wise
asleep	brought oil with their lamps. They all fell waiting for the bridegroom.
Go	At midnight someone yelled, "The bridegroom is coming. out to meet
young	him." All the women got up and cut the wicks on their lamps. The
oil	foolish ones asked the wise ones for some, but the wise women
for	couldn't give them any because there would not be enough everyone.
oil	The foolish young women left to buy some. While they were gone,
came	the bridegroom. The ones who were ready went inside for the wed-
door	ding, and the was shut behind them. When the foolish young women
the	returned, bridegroom didn't let them inside. He said, "I don't know
day	you." Jesus said for us to watch because we don't know the or hour when He'll come.

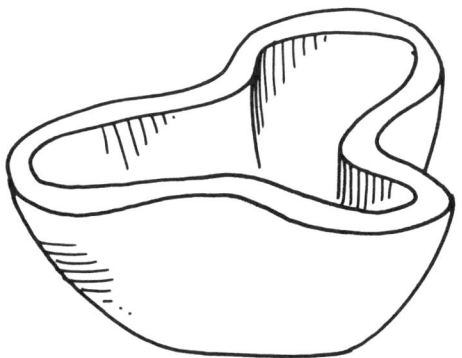

Just as the wise women were ready and waiting for the bridegroom, we can be ready by trusting Jesus as Lord and Savior.

You can make a lamp from clay like the one that Jesus might have been thinking about when He told this story. Keep your lamp in a spot where it will remind you to keep Jesus' light in your life.

Draw a star in this box when you've read Matthew 25:1-13.

The Christ

The Greek word "christ" means "anointed." When someone is anointed, oil is put on that person. Sometimes when people are anointed, it is to show that God has chosen that person for a special purpose, such as becoming a prophet, priest, or king. God chose Jesus to do something no one else could do—take the punishment for our sins and make us ready to live with God forever.

As Christians we get our name from Christ. We are people who believe Jesus is the Christ, the Anointed One. He is our Prophet, Priest, and King.

What is usually used to anoint? Write your answer on the drop.

Make a Bumper Sticker for Your Bike

What You Need
- white Con-Tact paper
- scissors
- permanent markers
- permission from a parent to put the sticker on your bike

What You Do

1. Be sure you are a Christian. Have you believed and done what is written at the bottom of this page?
2. If you are a Christian, make a bumper sticker by cutting a strip of white Con-Tact paper to fit on your bike.
3. Use permanent markers to write "I'm a Christian" and draw a cross on the Con-Tact paper.
4. Stick it onto your bike's fender.
5. When people ask you about your bumper sticker, tell them it means that you believe you are going to heaven because Jesus died for you and that you have promised to obey Him as your Lord. Tell them how they can become Christians, too.

How to Become a Christian

1. Believe that Jesus is the Christ and want Him to save you and lead you.
2. Pray a prayer like this in your own words:

Dear God,
I believe that Jesus is the Christ. Thank You for sending Him to save me from my sins. I am sorry for the things that I have done wrong. Please forgive me because of Jesus. I have faith in Him as my Savior, and I want to follow Him all of my life as my Lord.
In Jesus' name I pray. Amen.

Draw a star in this box when you've read Acts 4:27; 10:38; and Hebrews 1:9.

Commander

It's hard to win a battle if you don't even know you're fighting! Did you know you're in a war? The devil is your enemy. He uses different ways to tempt you to sin, and he tries to prevent you from doing the good that God wants you to do.

Jesus is leading His troops in the battle. In the Bible He is called the Commander of the army of the Lord, a Leader and Commander of the peoples, and the Deliverer.

You're one of His troops if you've asked Him to be your Lord. Listen to Jesus when He tells you how to fight temptations. Obey His commands. In order to win a battle, soldiers in the army need to listen to and obey the instructions of their leader. For Christians to win the war against Satan, we must listen to and obey the directions of our Commander.

Make Military I.D. Tags

People in some armies wear metal tags called "dog tags" to identify themselves.

What You Need
- 3" x 5" index card
- ruler
- pencil
- scissors
- small alphabet macaroni
- glue
- aluminum foil
- hole punch
- 26-inch piece of string
- tape

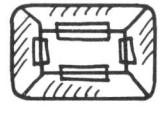

What You Do

1. Use a ruler to draw a rectangle about 1 inch by 2 inches on the 3" x 5" card. Fold the card in half and cut out two rectangles at the same time. Round the corners of each rectangle so both have a dog tag shape.

2. Arrange macaroni letters to say "I'm in the Lord's army" and glue them onto one dog tag. Arrange letters to spell your name and glue them onto the other dog tag. Let them dry.

3. Cover the dog tags with foil. Tape the foil to the back, and carefully rub your finger over the letters on the front so they show.

4. Punch a hole in each dog tag and hang them both from the string. Tie the ends of the string into a knot and put the dog tag necklace over your head to show that you're in the army of the Lord!

☐ *Draw a star in this box when you've read Joshua 5:13-15; Isaiah 55:4; Romans 11:26; and Ephesians 6:10-12.*

The Chief Cornerstone

If you were going to build a building, the first thing you must have is a foundation. The foundation of the building is the flat part on which the rest of the building is built. The chief cornerstone is the first rock that is put in the foundation and is a very important rock because the building won't stand if the other rocks don't fit with it.

The Lord's church is like a building made of people, and when God built His church, He knew He needed an incredibly perfect cornerstone. Jesus came to earth to be that cornerstone. Even though most of the Jewish leaders and lots of other people didn't believe in Him, He knew and God knew that the church couldn't stand without Him!

Fill in the Foundation

Jesus is the Chief Cornerstone of the house of God, and the rest of the foundation is the apostles and prophets. The things we believe should be based on what they have taught. How many disciples' and prophets' names can you fill in on this foundation? There are many more disciples and prophets than this in the real foundation of God's church, but here are some of them.

J_m_s   J_h_   Th_m_s   Ma_ _hew   P_u_

E_ij_h   J_n_h   D_ni_l   J_h_   P_t_r

J_su_   N_ _h   J_seph   M_s_s   Da_i_

You are one of the rocks of Jesus' church. Do you fit with the Cornerstone? Ask yourself these questions to find out.

1. Do the things I believe match what Jesus, the disciples, and the prophets really taught?
2. Am I letting Jesus make me more like Him each day?

Draw a star in this box when you've read Matthew 21:42; Mark 12:10; Luke 20:17; Acts 4:11; I Corinthians 3:11; Ephesians 2:19-22; and I Peter 2:6.

Friend

Jesus, the Son of God and Savior of the world, wants to be your friend! To decode what Jesus said about being a friend to you, find each friend's face at the top of the chart and the pattern on his or her shirt at the side of the chart. The column and the row meet at the letter you should write below the friend in the puzzle. For example, 😊 is A.

CODE

	A	E	I	M	R	V
	B	F	J	N	S	W
	C	G	K	O	T	Y
	D	H	L	P	U	Z

1. Jesus said, " _ ." (John 15:15)

2. If you feel too guilty to pray, remember: _ _ _ _ _ _ _ _ _ _ _ _ _ _ _ _ _ _ . (Luke 15:1-2)

3. Jesus showed how greatly He loves you, His friend, when _ _ _ _ _ _ _ _ _ _ _ _ ." (John 15:13)

4. You are never alone because Jesus said, " _ _ _ _ _ _ _ _ _ _ _ ." (Matt. 28:20)

☐ *Draw a star in this box when you've read Matthew 28:20; Luke 15:1, 2; and John 15:13, 15.*

The Gate

At night during the cold season, shepherds brought their sheep through a door or gate into a village sheepfold. Everyone, man or sheep, who wanted to enter the safety of the sheepfold had to go through that one door.

Jesus said, "I am the gate; whoever enters through me will be saved." Just as there was only one way to get into the sheepfold, there is only one way for us to get to heaven—Jesus.

Color the sheep with the letters B, D, W, and Z on them. The white sheep will tell you Jesus' message.

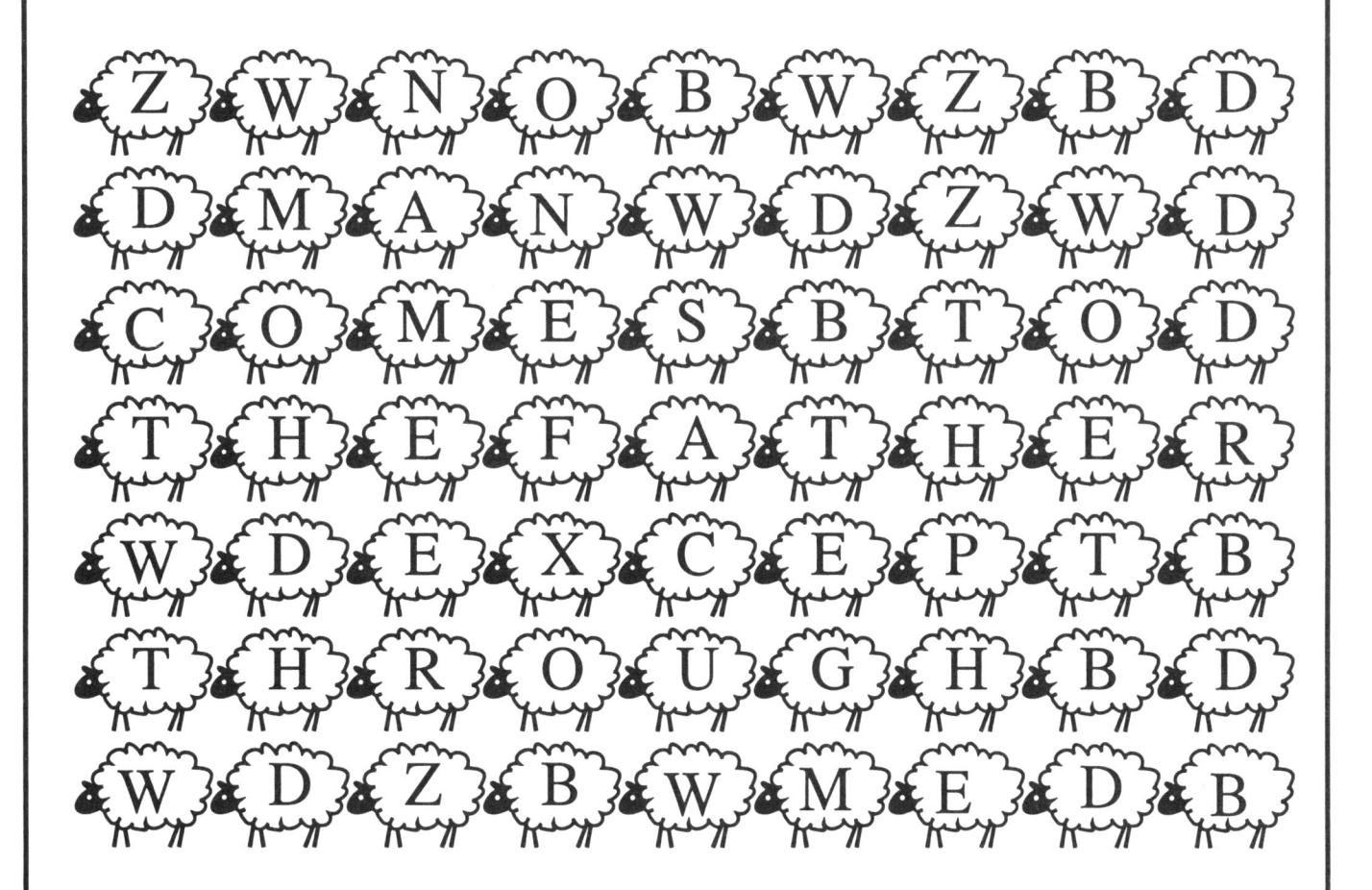

Z W N O B W Z B D
D M A N W D Z W D
C O M E S B T O D
T H E F A T H E R
W D E X C E P T B
T H R O U G H B D
W D Z B W M E D B

Draw a star in this box when you've read John 10:9 and 14:6.

The Gate and Ladders

Jesus said, "I tell you the truth, the man who does not enter the sheep pen by the gate, but climbs in by some other way, is a thief and a robber."

Even though Jesus told us clearly that He is the only way to heaven, people still try all kinds of other ways to get there. Cut out the beliefs at the bottom of the page. Most of them include things that are good to do, but only one of them will save you. Tape the false ideas on the ladders and the true one on the door.

Have you gone through Jesus to enter the kingdom of God? If you have asked Jesus to be your Savior, write your name on one of the sheep in the fold. If you aren't one of His sheep yet, you can become one by putting your trust in Jesus as the only way to get to heaven.

Beliefs to cut out and tape to the ladders and door.

| Being a nice person will save me. | Being a member of my church will save me. | Trusting the leaders of my church will save me. | Attending church will save me. | Being part of a good family will save me. | Trusting Jesus as my way to heaven will save me. |

Draw a star in this box when you've read John 10:1.

Gift of God

Everyone loves to get gifts, and God gave us the best gift of all! To find out more about God's gift, decode the answers to the questions below by finding the letter that has the same pattern as the wrapping paper on each gift.

1. When Jesus talked to the woman at the well, He spoke of Himself as what? (John 4:10)

2. Why was God willing to give His one and only son? (John 3:16)

3. A wage is something you earn, but a gift is something given to you. The wage of sin is death, but what is the gift of God? (Romans 6:23)

4. What is our response to God for the gift He's given us? (II Corinthians 9:15)

Draw a star in this box when you've read John 3:16; 4:10; Romans 6:23; and II Corinthians 9:15.

God

A name is a very important thing; it identifies a person. For the Jewish people, the name of God was a *very, very* special name. God told Moses His very special name. Many years later, Jesus called Himself the same name that God had told Moses. By doing that, Jesus said that He was God. What was the name that God had called Himself? *Color all of the spaces with dots to find this name.*

1. Circle the number that fills in the blank.
   Jesus said He and His Father are _____. (John 10:30)

   1   2   3   4   5   6   7   8   9   0

2. Circle the sign that fills in the blank.
   Some Jewish people tried to kill Jesus for saying that God was His Father, making Himself ____ with God. (John 5:18)

   +   -   =   < >

Draw a star in this box when you've read Exodus 3:13, 14; John 5:18; 8:58, 59; and 10:30.

Immanuel

Before Jesus was born, an angel appeared to Joseph in a dream and said that Jesus would be named Immanuel. *To find the meaning of the name in the puzzle below, find the letter each heart is beside. Write it in the box at the bottom of the column. When you have written the letters for all of the hearts, you'll have the meaning of the name Immanuel.*

A B C D E F G H I J K L M N O P Q R S T U V W X Y Z

Immanuel means ___ ___ ___   ___ ___ ___ ___

Draw a star in this box when you've read Matthew 1:23.

Jesus

Fill in the blanks and then write your answers in the squares of the puzzle at the bottom of the page. If your answers are right, you will find Jesus' name in the puzzle. When you find it, circle it.

1. "Jesus" is the Greek form of the Hebrew name _ _ _ _ _ _. God chose a man by this name to lead the children of Israel into the promised land of Canaan. The sixth book of the Old Testament is named after him.

2. An _ _ _ _ _ told Joseph in a dream that he should name God's son Jesus.

3. Jesus' name means "The LORD is _ _ _ _ _ _ _ _ _." (The last word of Luke 2:30)

4. This apostle wrote in Philippians 2:9 that Jesus' name is a name above every name. (Look at the first page of Philippians to see who wrote it.)
_ _ _ _

5. Jesus is the only name by which people must be _ _ _ _ _. (Acts 4:12).

Draw a star in this box when you've read Matthew 1:20, 21; Luke 2:30; Acts 4:12; and Philippians 2:9.

Make "Stained Glass" for Your Window

What You Need
- colored plastic food wrap (if unavailable, color plain plastic food wrap with permanent markers)
- paper plate
- glue
- string
- scissors
- thread
- tape

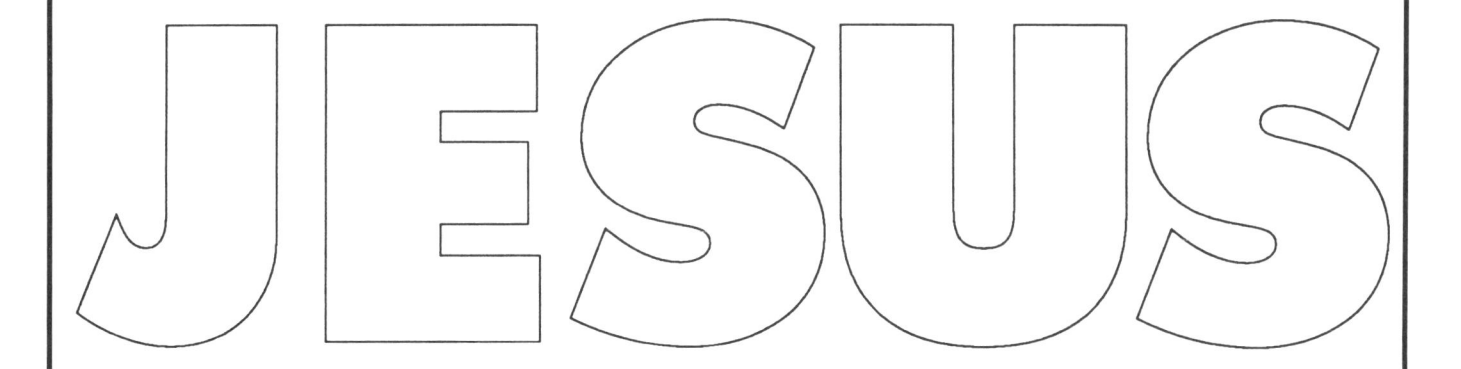

JESUS

What You Do
1. Tape colored plastic food wrap over the design on this page.
2. Measure and cut a piece of string to cover the lines on the letter "J."
3. Place the string on the plate and cover it with glue.
4. Carefully lay the string on top of the plastic wrap along the lines of the letter.
5. Cut and glue more strings for the rest of the letters in Jesus' name.
6. Let the letters dry completely.
7. Untape the plastic wrap from the page and trim the extra plastic wrap from around each letter.
8. Cut a tiny hole at the top of each letter.
9. Tie a thread through each hole. Hang the letters in your window by taping the threads to the window frame.

   •Variation—If you have more than one color of plastic wrap, you could make the letters different colors.

The King of Kings

What do you think of when you hear the word "power"? A president? A very rich man? A superhero? God gave Jesus incredible power and authority. Jesus has more power and authority than any king, president, or superhero.

Even though Jesus could force people to obey Him, He lets them choose whether they will or not. Christians are people who choose to let Jesus rule their lives. When people choose to follow Jesus, they become part of His kingdom.

Jesus told many stories of what His kingdom is like. *Write the number of the parable next to the picture it matches.*

1. A man who sowed (planted) good seed. (Matthew 13:24-30, 38-43)
2. A grain of a mustard seed. (Mark 4:30-32)
3. Leaven, yeast, or another substance that makes dough get light and fluffy. (Luke 13:20, 21)
4. A treasure. (Matthew 13:44)
5. A pearl. (Matthew 13:45, 46)
6. A net. (Matthew 13:47-50)

Draw a star in the box when you've read one of the Bible stories about Jesus' kingdom.

A Fun Thing to Do

You can write a book! Find and read one of Jesus' stories about His kingdom. Staple papers together to make a little book. Write the story in the book and illustrate it.

7. A king who forgave a man who owed him money until that man wouldn't forgive another. (Matthew 18:23-35)
8. A man who hired people to work in his grape vineyard at different times in the day and paid them all the same wage. (Matthew 20:1-16)
9. A king who gave a wedding feast for his son. (Matthew 22:2-14)
10. Ten young women with lamps. (Matthew 25:1-13)
11. A man leaving on a trip who gave his workers coins called talents (Matthew 25:14-30)

The Lamb of God

Before Jesus had died for our sins, God's people sacrificed perfect lambs to God. The lambs were killed for the people's sins. Men called High Priests took the lamb's blood into a room of the temple called the Holy of Holies. One name for Jesus is the Lamb of God. He was the absolutely perfect sacrifice and died for all the sins of the whole world. He acted as the last High Priest for us and went into God's presence to offer Himself as a sacrifice. Because Jesus did this, we no longer need to make sacrifices to God to get rid of our sin—we just ask for forgiveness!

Make a Peanut Lamb

This lamb can remind you to have faith that Jesus offered Himself as a sacrifice to take away your sins.

What You Need

- 2 peanuts (one with 2 nuts inside, one with 1 nut inside, see illustration)
- black pipe cleaner (chenille wire)
- scissors
- glue
- cotton balls
- black marker
- typing correction fluid or white paint

What You Do

1. Use the marker to color the face part of the small peanut. Dot correction fluid or paint on the face for eyes.
2. Cut the pipe cleaner into pieces that will be the lamb's 2 ears, neck, 4 legs, and tail.
3. Poke holes in the peanuts where the pipe cleaners will be. Bend the pipe cleaners to look like legs, ears, a neck, and a tail. Glue the pipe cleaners in the holes.
4. Glue on pieces of cotton balls to look like the picture.
5. Put your lamb where you can see it. Remember how much God loves you whenever you look at it!

Draw a star in this box when you've read John 1:29; Hebrews 9:7, 11-14.

The Light

Have you ever tried to look for something in the dark? You probably stumbled around and bumped into things. You may have even gotten hurt or lost!

Sin is like being in darkness. People who are sinning are lost in the dark. Jesus said that they don't know where they are going. They are looking for happiness, but they can't find it. Sin and evil thrive in darkness, but they can't stay where there is light.

How do you feel when the sun is shining on you? Warm? At peace? Jesus said, "I am the light of the world. Whoever follows me will never walk in darkness, but will have the light of life." He said, "I have come into the world as a light, so that no one who believes in me should stay in darkness."

Make a Switch Plate Cover

What happens to darkness when you turn on the light? What happens to evil and sin when you let Jesus light up your life?

What You Need
- crayons or paint and paintbrushes
- scissors
- tape

What You Do

1. Color or paint the switch plate cover on this page. You can even decorate it to match your room!

2. Cut out the switch plate cover. (Be careful when you cut out the rectangle in the middle.)

3. Tape your new switch plate over the switch plate in your room. Each time you turn on your light, remember that Jesus can fill your life with light.

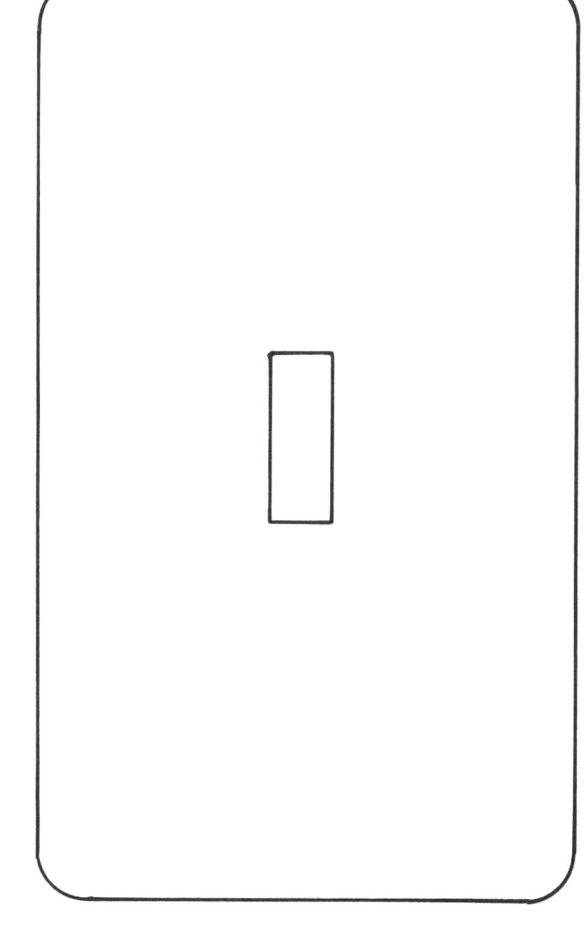

☐ *Draw a star in this box when you've read John 1:4, 5, 9; 3:19-21; 8:12; 12:35, 36, 46.*

The Lord

Calling Jesus your Lord means that you want to live your life however He wants you to. When you ask Him to be your Lord, you are saying that you want Him to be your master and that you will obey Him.

Jesus said, "Whoever loses his life for my sake will find it." If we leave our sinful life and decide to trust Jesus as Savior and Lord, He gives us life forever with God.

Jesus asked, "Why do you call me 'Lord, Lord,' and do not do what I say?" Then He told this story to show that when we have Jesus, the Rock, as the base of our lives, we can stand up to the troubles that come our way without being knocked down and out.

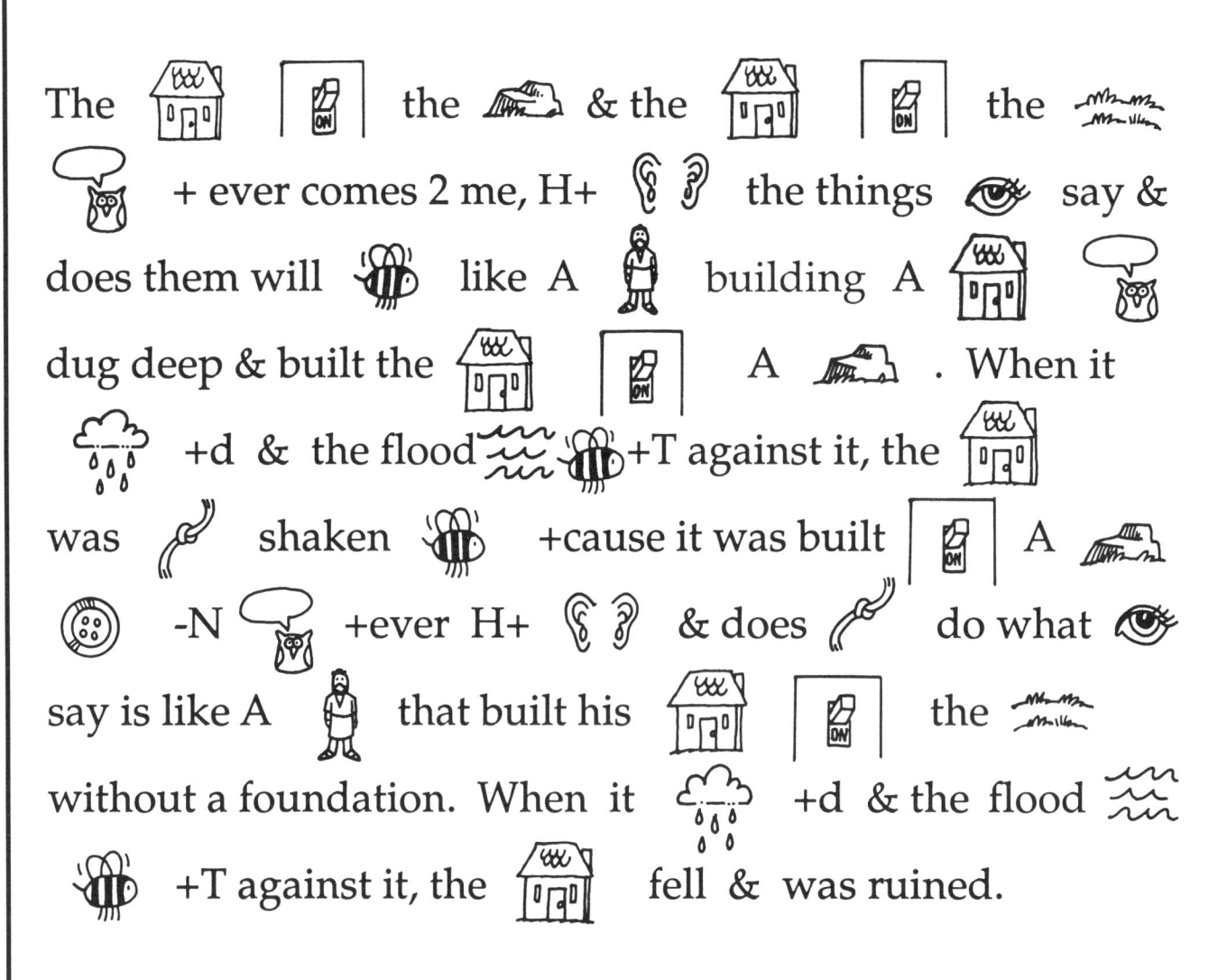

The 🏠 [ON] the 🪨 & the 🏠 [ON] the 🌾 🦉 + ever comes 2 me, H+ 👂👂 the things 👁 say & does them will 🐝 like A 🧔 building A 🏠 🦉 dug deep & built the 🏠 [ON] A 🪨. When it 🌧 +d & the flood 〰 🐝 +T against it, the 🏠 was 🚫 shaken 🐝 +cause it was built [ON] A 🪨. 🔘 -N 🦉 +ever H+ 👂👂 & does 🚫 do what 👁 say is like A 🧔 that built his 🏠 [ON] the 🌾 without a foundation. When it 🌧 +d & the flood 〰 🐝 +T against it, the 🏠 fell & was ruined.

☐ *Draw a star in this box when you've read Matthew 10:39; Mark 8:34-37; Luke 6:46-49; 9:23, 24.*

A House on a Rock

Ask Jesus to be your Lord. Live your life by what He says in the Bible and by what you learn when you pray, then you'll be building your "house" on a "rock"!

Can you draw this house without lifting your pencil and without redrawing any of the lines?

Draw Here

Jesus is my Lord and I will obey Him.

When you can draw this house without lifting your pencil, dip a single piece of twine in glue and glue it to a rock in the shape of a house. Write "Jesus is my Lord, and I will obey Him." on the rock with a permanent marker.

The Mediator

Have you ever had two friends who had a problem come between them? If you helped them work it out and get back together, you were a mediator. Sin has come between God and us. Jesus is the mediator who gets us back together with God.

Before Adam and Eve disobeyed God, they walked with God in the Garden of Eden. But then they disobeyed and sin entered the world and got between God and us. Jesus came to get sin out of the way so we could be with God. You can see how this works by using pepper, soap, and matches in a bowl of water.

Show How Jesus Gets Rid of Sin

What You Need
- help from an adult to use matches
- burned-out matches
- plastic knife
- Ivory soap
- pen
- two 3" x 5" index cards
- tape
- bowl
- shaker of black pepper
- red tissue or construction paper

How You Prepare
1. Use a plastic knife to carve a scrap of Ivory soap (it floats) into a cross.
2. Write "GOD" on an index card. Tape it inside a bowl so that most of the card sticks up outside of the bowl (see the picture).
3. Fill the bowl with water.
4. Write "SIN" on half of an index card and tape it to a can or shaker of black pepper.
5. Ask a grown-up to burn the tips of 2 matches and dip them in water so they're safe for you. DO NOT light the matches yourself!
6. Tape a piece of red paper shaped like a flame to one of the matches. It represents a "NEW PERSON." The other burned-out match represents a "SINFUL PERSON."

What You Do
You can show your family and friends how Jesus gets rid of our sin.
1. Sin separates people from God. (Sprinkle pepper between the "GOD" card and "SINFUL PERSON" match.)
2. When a person trusts Jesus as the only way to be saved, that person is born again and can be "on fire" for God. (Throw away burned-out "SINFUL PERSON" match. Put "NEW PERSON" match on cross.)
3. Jesus gets rid of sin that separates us from God. (Place cross in water and pepper will quickly float away from it.)
4. Jesus takes us to God. (Blow on cross until it floats over to the "GOD" card.)

Draw a star in this box when you've read Romans 5:11, 18; and I Timothy 2:5.

The Messiah

Do you remember what the Greek name "Christ" means? "Messiah" is a Hebrew name that means the same thing. *To find the meaning in the puzzle, start with the "A," skip the next letter, and write the letter after that. Continue around the drop of oil. When you get back to the A, write the letter following it and continue around the drop again. When you are finished, you will have the meaning of the name Messiah.*

```
    A
  T   E
E       N
          D
N         O
  N     O
    I
```

Jesus Fulfilled the Prophecies

The Jewish people were waiting for the Messiah to come. They had lots of descriptions of what He would be like from the prophecies of the Old Testament. (A prophecy is often a message from God that tells about something that will happen in the future.) Every one of those prophecies were true of Jesus. Some of them were about when He came to earth the first time, and some were about when He will come back, but they were all about Him. *Unscramble some of them.*

Prophecy: Micah 5:2
Fulfilled: Matthew 2:1-6

1. Born in HETBELMEH.

Prophecy: Zechariah 9:9
Fulfilled: Matthew 21:1-9

2. Rode into Jerusalem on a NEKYOD.

Prophecy: Psalm 22:16-18
Fulfilled: Matthew 27:35

3. Died on a SRSOC.

Prophecy: Isaiah 53:12
Fulfilled: Matthew 27:38

4. Suffered with BORREBS.

Prophecy: Psalm 69:21
Fulfilled: Mark 15:36

5. Offered a drink of GARVINE.

Prophecy: Psalm 16:10
Fulfilled: Matthew 28:5, 6

6. Raised from the EDAD.

☐ *Draw a star in this box when you have read each of the prophesies and fulfillments listed on this page.*

The Great Physician

Jesus is called the Great Physician because He makes people well. Can you fill in the blanks? You can find the answers in the Bible verses.

1. This man's friends lowered him through the roof to get him to Jesus. Jesus made him able to walk. What else did Jesus do for him?

F _ _ _ _ _ _ _ _ _ _ _ _ _ S (Luke 5:17-25)

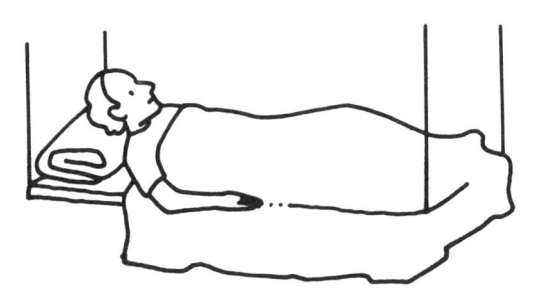

2. Who were three dead people Jesus brought back to life?

L _ _ _ _ _ S (John 11: 38-44)

The S _ _ of a _ _ _ _ W (Luke 7:11-15)

The D _ _ _ _ _ _ _ of _ _ _ _ _ S (Mark 5:21-24, 35-43)

3. Jesus healed the blind eyes of a beggar named

B _ _ _ _ _ _ _ _ S. (Mark 10:46-52)

4. Jesus healed Peter's mother-in-law, who had a

F _ _ _ R. (Matthew 8:14, 15)

5. When Jesus healed 10 lepers, only one came back to

T _ _ _ _ _ _ M. (Luke 17:11-19)

Draw a star in this box when you've read Matthew 8:14, 15; 9:1-8; Mark 5:21-23; 5:35-43; 10:46-52; Luke 7:11-18; 17:11-19; John 11:1-53.

The Redeemer

People once bought and sold other people. A slave was a person whom someone else owned, and who had to do whatever the owner said. Often a slave's only ticket to freedom was if he could find a redeemer. A redeemer was someone who bought a slave to set him free. The payment was called a ransom.

Sin makes people slaves; they aren't free to do what will really make them happy. They keep doing wrong things that make their lives hard and miserable. But Jesus paid his blood as a ransom to free people from sin. When people believe the truth about Jesus, they are set free.

Make a Ransom Note

A kidnapper is someone who takes a person away from those who love him. The kidnapper sometimes writes a "ransom note" asking for money to let that person go. The kidnapped person is not freed until someone who loves him pays the price (the ransom).

You can make your own ransom note. Just cut out letters and words from old magazines and newspapers to spell the message on this ransom note. Paste them onto this page.

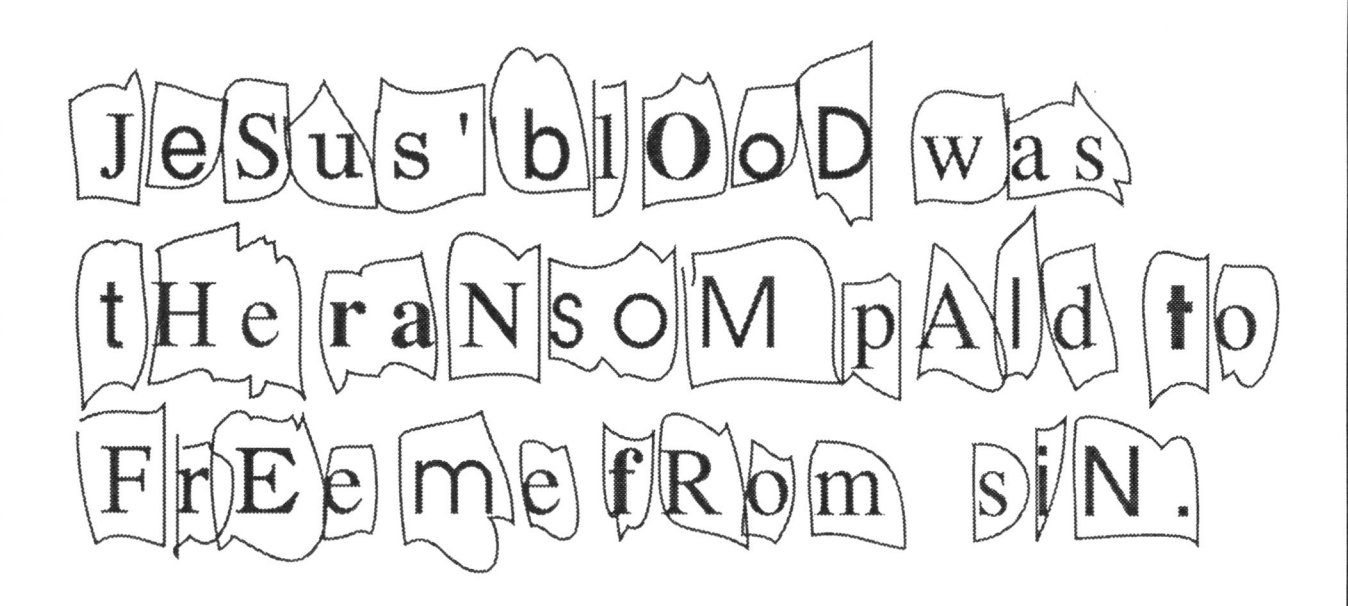

Jesus' blood was the ransom paid to free me from sin.

Draw a star in this box when you've read Matthew 20:28; Mark 10:45; John 8:31, 32, 34, 36; I Timothy 2:6.

The Resurrection and the Life

Jesus said, "I am the resurrection and the life. He who believes in me will live, even though he dies; and whoever lives and believes in me will never die."

The word "resurrect" means to raise from the dead. Because of Jesus, we will be raised from the dead after our bodies die. The life He gives us when we believe in Him is eternal—it will never end. Because Jesus died on the cross for you, your spirit can live with Him in heaven forever.

Decode this puzzle. In the blank below each picture, write the first letter of the word that begins the picture.

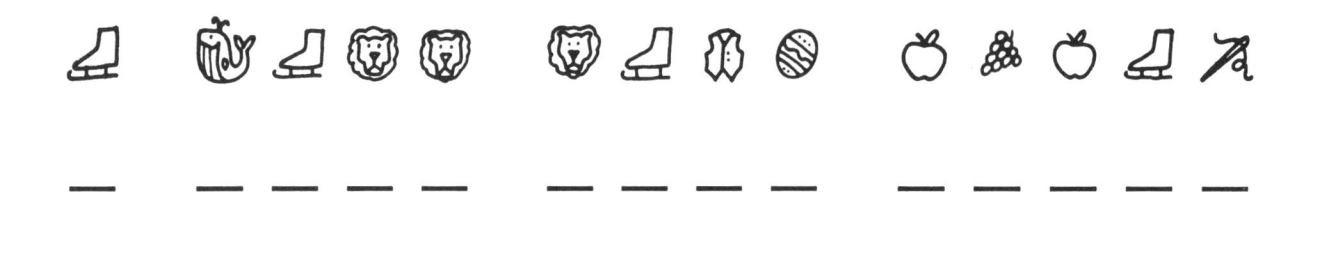

_ _ _ _ _   _ _ _ _   _ _ _ _ _

_ _ _ _ _ _ _   _ _ _ _   _ _ _ _

_ _ _ _ _ _ _   _ _   _ _ _ _ _.

Draw a star in this box when you've read John 11:25, 26.

The Rock

Find and circle the letters of JESUS on the rock. Find and circle the letters of HOLY SPIRIT in the water.

In Old Testament times Moses and the Israelites came to a place in the desert where there wasn't anything to drink, so God gave them water out of a rock. That rock was like Jesus.

Jesus told a woman at a well, "Whoever drinks the water I give him will never thirst. Indeed, the water I give him will become in him a spring of water welling up to eternal life."

Jesus also said at another time, "If anyone is thirsty, let him come to me and drink. Whoever believes in me, as the Scripture has said, streams of living water will flow from within him." The living water that Jesus was talking about is the Holy Spirit. People who believe in Jesus receive the Holy Spirit.

Have you ever been terribly thirsty? Just like our bodies get thirsty for water, our spirits get thirsty for God. When you come to Jesus, the Rock, and believe in Him as your Savior, He will fill you with the living water of the Holy Spirit.

Draw a star in this box when you've read John 4:13, 14; 7:37-39; and I Corinthians 10:4.

35

The Savior

When a person is in major trouble, it is sometimes called being in "deep water." Sin is the deepest water we can get into, but putting your faith in Jesus is like taking hold of a lifesaver that can pull you out of danger.

Take Hold of the Lifesaver

A gift is not something that you earn. It is given free of charge. Salvation is a gift from God, and He wants you to accept it like you would accept any present—just take it. The life preserver is being held out to you and all you have to do is hold onto it. There is only one name on the life preserver that can save you. The name that saves is Jesus.

To be saved, believe that Jesus is the Son of God, that He died to take the punishment for your sins, and that He lives again. Trust Him as the only way for you to get to heaven, and promise to follow Him as your Lord.

To Accept Jesus as Your Savior and Lord, Pray a Prayer Like This in Your Own Words:

Dear God,
I love You. I know that I don't deserve to live with You because of anything I have done, but I am thankful that You offer eternal life to me as a free gift because of Your Son, Jesus. I believe He is who He said He was. Please forgive my sins because He died for me. I am putting my trust in Him as my Savior and I will follow Him as my Lord all of my life. Thank You for saving me.
In Jesus' name I pray. Amen.

Make a Lifesaver Pendant

To let others know how glad you are that Jesus saved you, you can make this pendant. When people notice you wearing it, explain to them how Jesus is your lifesaver. If they want to be saved, too, help them pray a prayer like the one on this page.

Draw a star in this box when you've read Matthew 10:22; 24:13; Acts 4:12; Romans 10:9, 10, 13; and Ephesians 2:8.

Servant

After the Last Supper, Jesus washed each of the disciples' feet to show that He was willing to serve them. He said, "The greatest among you should be like the youngest, and the one who rules like the one who serves. For who is greater, the one who is at the table or the one who serves? Is it not the one who is at the table? But I am among you as one who serves." Jesus served us, and He wants us to serve each other.

Serve Your Family

Trace the right foot of each member of your family on colored paper. Cut out the paper feet and glue them onto a sheet of white paper. List things on each foot that you can do for that foot's owner this week.

If the rest of the family wants to get involved, make a foot picture for each of them to write on, too.

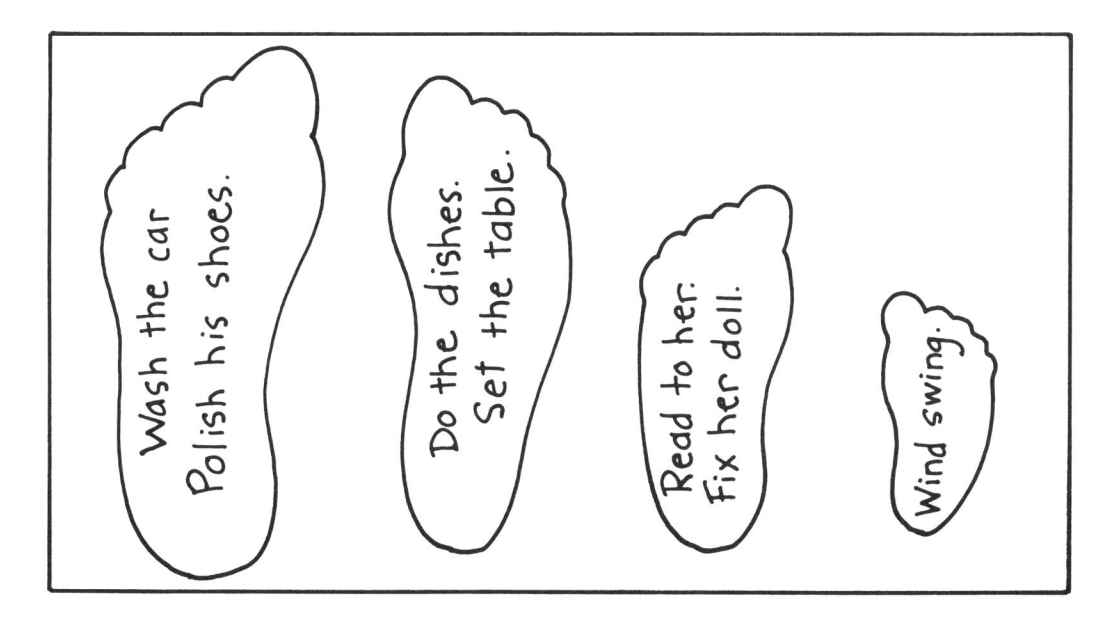

- Wash the car. Polish his shoes.
- Do the dishes. Set the table.
- Read to her. Fix her doll.
- Wind swing.

Draw a star in this box when you've read Luke 22:26, 27; and John 13:4-15.

The Good Shepherd

Jesus said, "I am the good shepherd; I know my sheep and my sheep know me—just as the Father knows me and I know the Father—and I lay down my life for the sheep. I have other sheep that are not of this sheep pen. I must bring them also. They too will listen to my voice, and there shall be one flock and one shepherd."

Jesus also said, "My sheep listen to my voice; I know them, and they follow me. I give them eternal life, and they shall never perish; no one can snatch them out of my hand. My Father, who has given them to me, is greater than all; no one can snatch them out of my Father's hand. I and the Father are one."

Make a Gumdrop Lamb and Shepherd

Use these candies to remind you to follow the Good Shepherd!

What You Need
- 10 gumdrops (4 white, 2 black, 2 pairs of any color)
- 9 toothpicks
- scissors
- food coloring

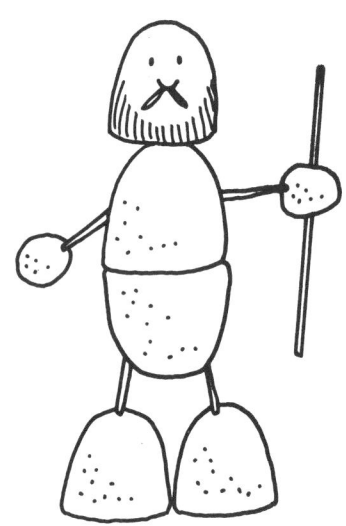

What You Do to Make the Shepherd
1. Cut four toothpicks in half with scissors. Don't break them; that could leave splinters.
2. Make a body by connecting two colored gumdrops with a toothpick half.
3. Use another toothpick half to stick a white gumdrop to the body for a head.
4. Stick a toothpick half on each side of the body for arms. Pinch two pieces off of a white gumdrop and stick one onto each arm for hands. Stick a whole toothpick through one of the hands for a shepherd's staff.
5. Stick two toothpick halves into the gumdrop body for legs, and stick a colored gumdrop at the end of each leg for feet. Adjust the toothpicks and gumdrops until the shepherd can stand.
6. Dip the tip of a whole toothpick in a drop of food coloring. Draw a face on the head. Let dry.

What You Do to Make the Lamb
1. Cut four toothpicks in half with scissors. Don't break them; that could leave splinters.
2. Connect two white gumdrops with a toothpick half to make a body.
3. Use a toothpick half to connect a black gumdrop to the body for a head.
4. Pinch a small piece off of a black gumdrop and attach it to the body with a toothpick half for a tail.
5. Stick four toothpick halves into the body for legs and adjust them until your sheep will stand.

Draw a star in this box when you've read John 10:14-16; 27-30.

The Son of God

Jesus' Father was God. When Jesus was baptized, God spoke from heaven and said, "This is my Son, whom I love; with him I am well pleased." Another time when God spoke from heaven about Jesus is called "The Transfiguration." Think about how you would have felt if you were there.

The Transfiguration

Change each BOLD, CAPITALIZED word to its opposite, and read this story.

One (1) **NIGHT** _____ Jesus took Peter, James, and John with Him (2) **DOWN** _____ a mountain to pray. As Jesus prayed, He started to look different. His face shone like the (3) **MOON** _____, and His clothes became as (4) **BLACK** _____ as light. Moses and Elijah, prophets from (5) **NEW** _____ Testament times, (6) **DISAPPEARED** _____ and talked with Jesus about his upcoming (7) **BIRTH** _____ in Jerusalem.

Peter said, "It is (8) **BAD** _____ for us to be (9) **THERE** _____. Let us put up three shelters—one for you, one for Moses, and one for Elijah." While (10) **SHE** ____ was talking, a (11) **DIM** _____ cloud covered them and a voice from the cloud said, "This is my Son whom I have chosen; listen to Him!"

Peter, James, and John fell flat (12) **OFF** ____ their faces and were terrified. Jesus came to them, touched them, and said, "Get up, and don't be afraid." When they looked (13) **DOWN** ____, they only saw Jesus. He was standing by Himself.

☐ *Draw a star in this box when you've read Matthew 3:17; 17:1-8; Mark 1:11, 9:2-8; Luke 9:28-36.*

39

The True Vine

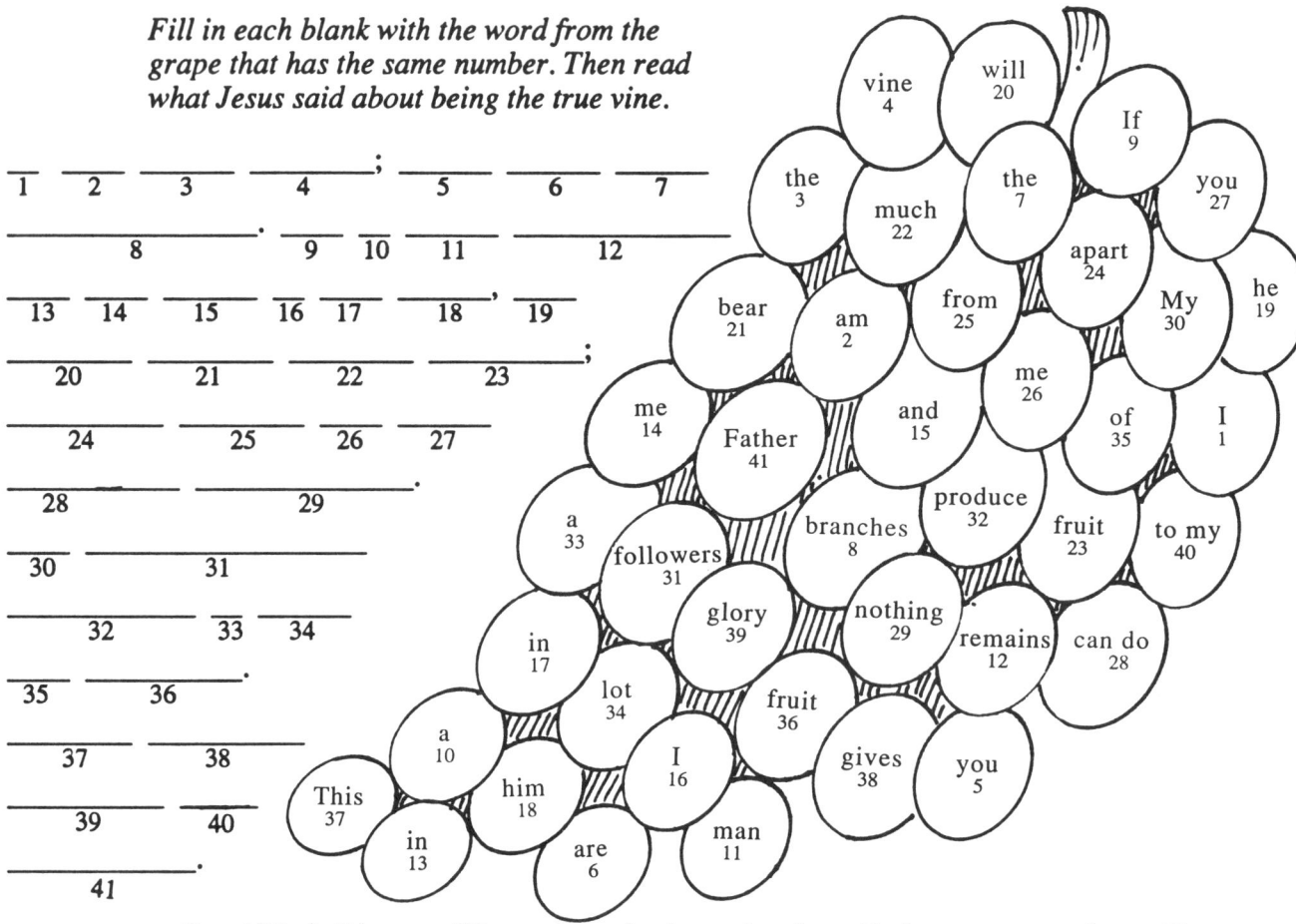

Fill in each blank with the word from the grape that has the same number. Then read what Jesus said about being the true vine.

$\underset{1}{I}$ $\underset{2}{am}$ $\underset{3}{the}$ $\underset{4}{vine}$; $\underset{5}{you}$ $\underset{6}{are}$ $\underset{7}{the}$ $\underset{8}{branches}$. $\underset{9}{If}$ $\underset{10}{a}$ $\underset{11}{man}$ $\underset{12}{remains}$ $\underset{13}{in}$ $\underset{14}{me}$ $\underset{15}{and}$ $\underset{16}{I}$ $\underset{17}{in}$ $\underset{18}{him}$, $\underset{19}{he}$ $\underset{20}{will}$ $\underset{21}{bear}$ $\underset{22}{much}$ $\underset{23}{fruit}$; $\underset{24}{apart}$ $\underset{25}{from}$ $\underset{26}{me}$ $\underset{27}{you}$ $\underset{28}{can\ do}$ $\underset{29}{nothing}$. $\underset{30}{My}$ $\underset{31}{followers}$ $\underset{32}{produce}$ $\underset{33}{a}$ $\underset{34}{lot}$ $\underset{35}{of}$ $\underset{36}{fruit}$. $\underset{37}{This}$ $\underset{38}{gives}$ $\underset{39}{glory}$ $\underset{40}{to\ my}$ $\underset{41}{Father}$.

Good "fruits" in your life are the attitudes and actions God wants you to have. If you have accepted Jesus, He is like a vine that feeds you and gives you everything you need to be who God wants you to be and do what God wants you to do.

When you produce good fruit, it glorifies God and shows that you are Jesus' follower. You are only able to do the good that Jesus wants you to do if you stay close to Him—branches can't grow grapes if they are pulled off the vine!

Bear Good Fruit

Pray and ask God what He would like you to do. Listen carefully and then write some of those things on these grapes. Ask the Lord to help you do the things that He wants you to do.

Jesus: The Vine

You: The Branches

Your Attitudes & Actions: The Grapes

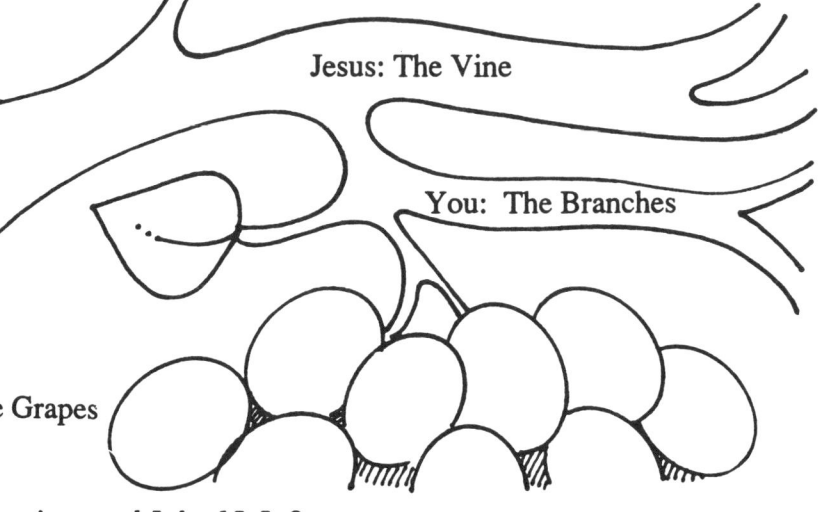

Draw a star in this box when you've read John 15:5, 8.

The Way

Jesus said, "I am the way and the truth and the life. No one comes to the Father except through me." You can't save yourself by doing good. Your church can't save you. Not even your parents can save you. Jesus is the only way to get to heaven. The Bible says, "it is by grace you have been saved, through faith—and this not from yourselves, it is the gift of God—not by works, so that no one can boast." Eternal life in Jesus is a free gift. All you have to do is accept it!

Make a Ladder That Shows the Way to God

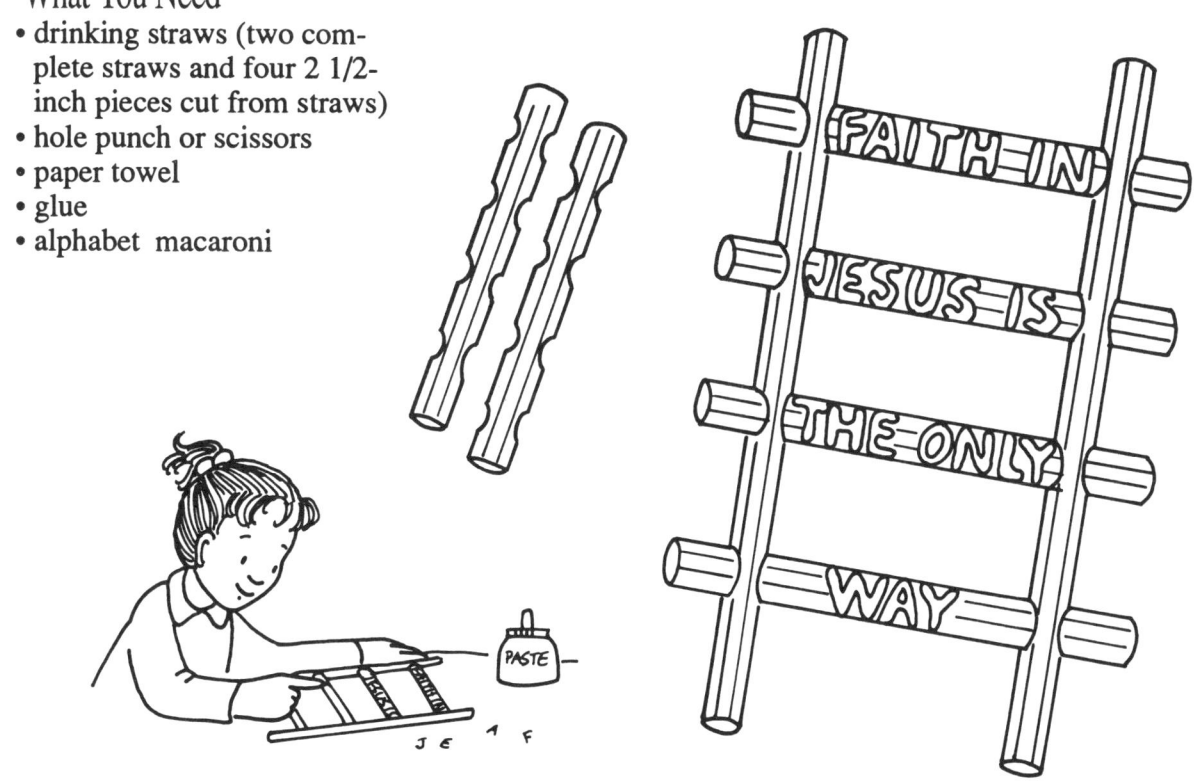

What You Need
- drinking straws (two complete straws and four 2 1/2-inch pieces cut from straws)
- hole punch or scissors
- paper towel
- glue
- alphabet macaroni

What You Do
1. Punch or cut four holes about an inch apart through both sides of a straw. Make sure that the holes are directly across from each other. Repeat with another straw.
2. Poke the straw pieces through the holes to make a ladder.
3. Lay the ladder on the paper towel and glue on alphabet letters that spell "Faith in Jesus is the only way."

Draw a star in this box when you've read John 14:6; and Ephesians 2:8, 9.

The Word

People use words to let others know what they are thinking. Jesus let us know what God thinks, so Jesus is called "The Word."

A Word Puzzle

There are some words from John 1:1-3 hidden in this puzzle. The words can go up and down, left and right, or diagonally.

Look for these words: WORD, BEGINNING, WERE, ALL, GOD, THINGS, MADE, HIM

```
S G N I H T J L F
L N Z O P Q L P N
T I K W E A H Y R
F N S E O M G I M
J N M L L R O E A
Y I I R A M D A D
E G H A B W R T E
D E L A W E R E A
M B E N A N D I L
```

Decide if the sentences below are true or false. Circle the letter under the correct answer for each sentence. If your answers are right, they will spell a word. (You can check your answers in John 1:1-3.)

	TRUE	FALSE
1. Jesus wasn't with God in the beginning.	R	W
2. Jesus was God.	O	A
3. Everything was made through Jesus.	R	K
4. Some things were made without Jesus.	L	D

Draw a star in this box when you've read John 1:1-3.

ANSWERS

Page 5

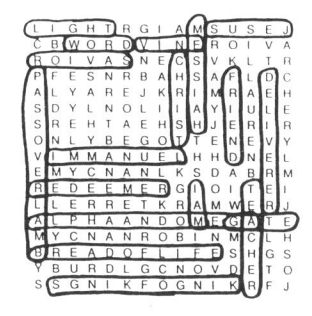

Page 6 1. Savior; 2. Messiah; 3. Bread of Life; 4. Friend; 5. God; 6. Lord; 7. Lamb of God; 8. King of Kings; 9. Word; 10. Redeemer

Page 8 1. People want to know God and be sure they will get to live with Him forever. When they put their trust in Jesus, He satisfies that hunger like the manna satisfied the hunger of the Israelites.
2. The Israelites would have died if God had not sent manna. We would all die for eternity if God had not sent Jesus.
3. The Israelites had to collect their manna every day. We need to pray every day and keep trusting in Jesus.

Page 10 1. service; 2. lamps; 3. wedding; 4. knocks; 5. door; 6. servants; 7. watching; 8. table; 9. good; 10. master

Page 12 The kingdom of heaven is like ∧ young women who took their lamps and went to meet the bridegroom. Five of them were ∧ and five were foolish. The foolish ones brought lamps without extra ∧, but the wise brought oil with their lamps. They all fell ∧ waiting for the bridegroom. At midnight someone yelled, "The bridegroom is coming. ∧ out to meet him." All the ∧ women got up and cut the wicks on their lamps. The foolish ones asked the wise ones for some ∧, but the wise women couldn't give them any because there would not be enough ∧ everyone. The foolish young women left to buy some ∧. While they were gone, the bridegroom ∧. The ones who were ready went inside for the wedding, and the ∧ was shut behind them. When the foolish young women returned, ∧ bridegroom didn't let them inside. He said, "I don't know you." Jesus said for us to watch because we don't know the ∧ or hour when He'll come.

Page 15 Beginning with top left picture: 1. James; 2. John; 3. Thomas; 4. Matthew; 5. Paul; 6. Elijah; 7. Jonah; 8. Daniel; 9. John; 10. Peter; 11. Jesus; 12. Noah; 13. Joseph; 14. Moses; 15. David

Page 16 1. Jesus said, "I have called you friends."
2. If you feel too guilty to pray, remember: Jesus was a friend of sinners.
3. Jesus showed how greatly He loves you, His friend, when He gave His life for you.
4. You are never alone because Jesus said, "I am with you always."

ANSWERS

Page 17 No man comes to the Father except through me.

Page 18 "Trusting Jesus as my way to heaven will save me." should be taped on the door.

Page 19 1. The gift of God; 2. He loved the world; 3. Eternal life; 4. Too wonderful for words

Page 20 Hidden name: I AM; 1. 1; 2. =

Page 21 God with us

Page 22 1. Joshua; 2. Angel; 3. Salvation; 4. Paul; 5. Saved

Pages 24-25 1. A; 2. C; 3. F; 4. I; 5. H; 6. J; 7. D; 8. B; 9. 3; 10. G; 11. K

Page 29

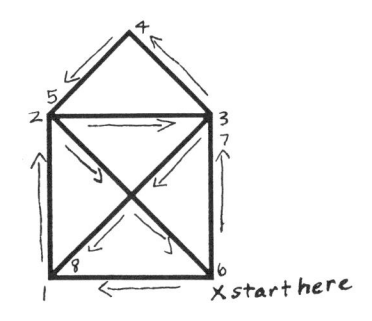

Page 31 Anointed One; 1. Bethlehem; 2. Donkey; 3. Cross; 4. Robbers; 5. Vinegar; 6. Dead

Page 32 1. Forgave his sins; 2. Lazarus, The son of a widow, The daughter of Jairus; 3. Bartimaeus; 4. Fever; 5. Thank Him

Page 34 I will live again after my body dies because of Jesus.

Page 35

Page 39 1. day; 2. up; 3. sun; 4. white; 5. Old; 6. appeared; 7. death; 8. good; 9. here; 10. he; 11. bright; 12. on; 13. up

Page 40 I am the vine; you are the branches. If a man remains in me and I in him, he will bear much fruit; apart from me you can do nothing. My followers produce a lot of fruit. This gives glory to my Father.

Page 42 1. False
2. True
3. True
4. False

44

I DID IT!

Life and Lessons of Jesus Series

COMPLETED		DATE	COMPLETED		DATE
☐	Seek and You Will Find	_____	☐	The Light	_____
☐	Add a Line	_____	☐	The Lord	_____
☐	Alpha and Omega	_____	☐	The Mediator	_____
☐	The Bread of Life	_____	☐	The Messiah	_____
☐	The Bridegroom	_____	☐	The Great Physician	_____
☐	The Christ	_____	☐	The Redeemer	_____
☐	Commander	_____	☐	The Resurrection and the Life	_____
☐	The Chief Cornerstone	_____	☐	The Rock	_____
☐	Friend	_____	☐	The Savior	_____
☐	The Gate	_____	☐	Servant	_____
☐	Gift of God	_____	☐	The Good Shepherd	_____
☐	God	_____	☐	The Son of God	_____
☐	Immanuel	_____	☐	The True Vine	_____
☐	Jesus	_____	☐	The Way	_____
☐	The King of Kings	_____	☐	The Word	_____
☐	The Lamb of God	_____			

Index of *The Life and Lessons of Jesus* Series

BOOKS
1. Jesus Is Born
2. Jesus Grows Up
3. Jesus Prepares to Serve
4. Jesus Works Miracles
5. Jesus Heals
6. Learning to Love Like Jesus
7. Jesus Teaches Me to Pray
8. Following Jesus
9. Jesus Shows God's Love
10. Names of Jesus
11. Jesus' Last Week
12. Jesus Is Alive!

BIBLE STORY	LIFE AND LESSONS
1st Miraculous Catch of Fish	Book 4
2nd Miraculous Catch of Fish	Books 4, 12
10 Disciples See Jesus	Book 12
Angels Visit Shepherds	Book 1
As Father Has Loved Me . . .	Books 9, 11
Ascension	Book 12
Ask in Jesus' Name	Book 11
Ask, Seek, Knock	Book 7
Baby Jesus at the Temple	Book 2
Baptism of Jesus	Book 3
Beatitudes	Books 6, 9
Becoming Child of God	Book 9
Belief and Baptism	Books 8, 12
Blind Leading Blind	Book 8
Boy Jesus at the Temple	Books 2, 3
Calming the Storm	Book 4
Careless Words	Book 6
Christian Christmas Ideas	Book 1
Christian Easter Story and Activities	Books 11, 12
Coin in Fish's Mouth	Book 4
Count the Cost	Book 8
Demons into Pigs	Book 5
Disciples Find a Donkey	Book 11
Divorce/Stay Married	Book 6
Do Not Let Your Heart Be Troubled	Book 11
Don't Insult Others	Book 6
Don't Worry About Food and Clothes	Books 7, 9
Endure to the End	Book 8
Escape to Egypt	Book 2
Extra Mile	Book 6
Faith of a Mustard Seed	Book 7
Faith to Move a Mountain	Book 7
Fasting	Book 7
Feed My Sheep	Book 12
Feeding the 5,000 and 4,000	Book 4
Forgive	Books 6, 7
Forgiven Much, Love Much	Book 9
Gabriel Visits Mary	Book 1
Garden of Gethsemane	Book 11
Get Rid of What Causes Sin	Book 8
Gift of Holy Spirit	Books 9, 12
Give and Lend	Book 6
Give to Caesar What Is Caesar's	Book 8
God and Money	Book 8
God Gives Good Gifts	Book 7
God Wants Us in Heaven	Book 9
Golden Rule	Book 6
Good Deeds in Secret	Book 8

BIBLE STORY	LIFE AND LESSONS
Great Commission	Book 12
Greatest Commandments	Books 6, 8
Greatest Is Servant	Book 6
Hairs Are Numbered	Book 9
Hand on Plow	Book 8
Healing at the Pool of Bethesda	Book 5
Healing of 10 Lepers	Book 5
Healing of a Blind Man	Book 6
Healing of a Deaf and Mute Man	Book 6
Healing of a Leper	Book 5
Healing of a Man's Hand	Book 5
Healing of Blind Bartimaeus	Book 5
Healing of Centurion's Servant	Book 5
Healing of Epileptic Boy	Book 5
Healing of Malchus's Ear	Book 5
Healing of Man Born Blind	Book 6
Healing of Man with Dropsy	Book 5
Healing of Official's Son	Book 5
Healing of Peter's Mother-in-Law	Book 5
Healing of the Paralytic	Book 5
Healing of the Woman's Back	Book 5
Healing of Woman Who Touched Hem	Book 5
Heaven	Book 12
How Much God Loves Us	Book 9
Humble Prayer	Book 7
I Am with You Always	Book 12
I Live/You Will Live	Book 11
Include Others	Book 6
Jesus Clears the Temple	Book 11
Jesus Died for Me	Book 9
Jesus Eats with Sinners	Book 9
Jesus Has Overcome the World	Book 11
Jesus Is 'I AM'	Book 10
Jesus Is Arrested	Book 11
Jesus Is Born	Books 1, 2
Jesus Is Buried	Book 11
Jesus Is Christ	Books 3, 10
Jesus Is Crucified and Dies	Book 11
Jesus Is God	Book 10
Jesus Is Immanuel	Book 10
Jesus Is Tempted	Book 3
Jesus Is the Bread of Life	Book 10
Jesus Is the Bridegroom	Book 10
Jesus Is the Chief Cornerstone	Book 10
Jesus Is the Gate	Book 10
Jesus Is the Gift of God	Book 10
Jesus Is the Good Shepherd	Book 10
Jesus Is the Lamb of God	Book 10
Jesus Is the Light	Book 10
Jesus Is the Redeemer	Book 10
Jesus Is the Resurrection and Life	Book 10
Jesus Is the Savior	Book 10

Index of *The Life and Lessons of Jesus* Series

BIBLE STORY	LIFE AND LESSONS
Jesus Is the Son of God	Book 10
Jesus Is the Truth	Book 10
Jesus Is the Vine	Book 10
Jesus Is the Way	Books 10, 11
Jesus Is the Word	Book 10
Jesus Loves Children	Book 9
Jesus Obeys Parents	Book 2
Jesus Prayed	Book 7
Jesus Shows Compassion	Book 9
Jesus Washes Disciples' Feet	Books 6, 10, 11
Jesus' Family	Book 2
Jesus' Genealogy	Book 1
Jesus' Trial Before Caiaphas	Book 11
Jesus' Trial Before Pilate	Book 11
John the Baptist	Book 3
Joseph's Dream	Book 1
Judas Betrays Jesus	Books 3, 11
Judge Not	Book 6
Known by Fruits	Book 8
Last Supper	Book 11
Lay Down Life for Friends	Books 8, 10, 11
Lazarus and the Rich Man	Book 8
Life in New Testament Times	Book 2
Light on a Hill	Book 8
Like Days of Noah	Book 12
Like Jonah's Three Days in Fish	Book 12
Lord's Prayer	Book 7
Love Each Other	Book 11
Love Jesus Most	Book 9
Love Me/Obey Me	Book 11
Love One Another	Book 8
Loving Enemies	Books 6, 7
Make Up Quickly	Book 6
Maps of New Testament Times	Books 1-5
Mary and Martha	Book 8
Mary Anoints Jesus with Perfume	Book 11
Mary Visits Elizabeth	Book 1
Name the Baby Jesus	Book 10
Narrow Road	Book 8
New Commandment: Love	Book 6
Nicodemus	Book 8
Not Left As Orphans	Book 11
Old and New Cloth	Book 8
Oxen in a Pit	Book 5
Parable of the Friend at Midnight	Book 7
Parable of the Good Samaritan	Book 6
Parable of the Lost Coin	Book 9
Parable of the Lost Sheep	Book 9
Parable of the Overpaid Workers	Book 8
Parable of the Persistent Widow	Book 7
Parable of the Prodigal Son	Books 7, 8
Parable of the Sheep and Goats	Books 6, 12
Parable of Sower and Seeds	Books 8, 10, 12
Parable of the Ten Young Women	Book 10

BIBLE STORY	LIFE AND LESSONS
Parable of the Unforgiving Servant	Book 6
Parable of Wedding Feast	Book 10
Parable of Weeds	Book 12
Parable of Wise and Foolish Builders	Book 10
Parables of Mustard Seed and Leaven	Books 10, 12
Parables of Treasure, Pearl, Fishnet	Books 10, 12
Passover	Books 2, 10, 11
Peter's Denial	Books 3, 11
Pharisee and Tax Collector at Temple	Book 6
Pharisees' Hypocrisy	Book 8
Pray Always	Book 7
Prepare a Place for You	Books 9, 11, 12
Promise of Holy Spirit	Book 11
Raising of Jairus's Daughter	Book 5
Raising of Lazarus	Book 5
Raising of Widow's Son	Book 5
Rich Toward God	Book 8
Rich Young Ruler	Book 8
Road to Emmaus	Book 12
Salt of the Earth	Book 8
Second Coming	Book 12
Seek Kingdom First	Book 7
Seventy Times Seven	Book 6
Sheep Know His Voice	Book 7
Shepherd Knows Sheep	Book 9
Speck and the Plank	Book 6
Spiritual Harvest	Book 8
Take Up Your Cross	Book 9
Thief in the Night	Book 12
Thomas Sees Resurrected Jesus	Book 12
Transfiguration	Book 3
Treasure in Heaven	Book 8
Triumphal Entry	Book 11
True Members of Jesus' Family	Book 2
Truth Makes You Free	Book 10
Twelve Disciples	Book 3
Two Agree in Prayer	Book 7
Under His Wing	Book 9
Vine and Branches	Book 10
Walking on Water	Book 4
Water to Wine	Book 4
What Makes a Person Unclean	Book 8
Widow's Mites	Book 8
Wine and Wineskins	Book 8
Wise Men Visit Jesus	Book 1
Withered Fig Tree	Book 4
Wolves in Sheep's Clothing	Book 8
Woman at the Well	Book 10
Woman Caught Sinning	Book 6
Worth More than Sparrows	Book 9
Yoke Easy, Burden Light	Book 7
Zaccheus	Book 9

If you would like to write the author, send your letter to:

Your address here

Stamp

Tracy L. Harrast
c/o Church Resources Dept.
David C. Cook Publishing Co.
850 N. Grove Avenue
Elgin, IL 60120